The Practical Re  of

Learning

A Simple Practical Guide

For Teachers, Parents,

Church Groups, Home School, Young Adults

Do-it Yourselfers, and Self-helpers

By

Dr. Myron Baughman

The Learning Series

While every precaution has been taken in the preparation of this book, the publisher assumes no responsibility for errors or omissions, or for damages resulting from the use of the information contained herein.

THE PRACTICAL RESOURCE BOOK

First edition. December 1, 2024.

Copyright © 2024 Myron Baughman.

ISBN: 979-8227991768

Written by Myron Baughman.

Also by Myron Baughman

Pneumasites
Pneumasites 2

The Learning Series
The Practical Resource Book

Zeb Dasher Mystery Novels
The Twisted Case of the Presidential Conspiracy
The Wizard's Haunted Castle Mystery

Standalone
Pneumasites
Educating Everett
My Puppy Theo
Trixie: The Pixie Angel
The Ghosts of Griswoldville

Watch for more at https://www.sermonaudio.com/
source_detail.asp?sourceid=kingjamesseminary.

This book is dedicated to my loving wife Denise

To the Reader:

I am Dr. Myron Baughman. I've taught grades from elementary up to and including graduate level for many years. In this book, I am laying out for any interested person, be it a teacher, parent, grandparent, home schooler, or Christian Educator, multiple helps that you may find useful in your guidance and teaching of children at different age levels. Keep in mind these are only helps and suggestions. This book may also be of use for the young adult, just starting out in life. If you will notice, there are no references in that I have typed this information from memory, and old lesson plans, having used these things repeatedly. As you know, for many things in life that you do, you don't need a reference guide This guide will be especially helpful in disputes in games, or moments of uncertainty. Yes, I have done all of these things in this book. There is no substitute for experience. The information given has been proof read, and is free of error. I will give a list of reference books at the back of this book that you may want to refer to for more and similar information than what I have given. I have not directly quoted any of these books, nor have even looked inside any of them, but they are on the subjects I cover, so maybe some of them will be of use to you beyond what I cover in this book. There are many valuable resources found on the internet also that you should check out. All of the games, and activities I have personally participated in, taught and coached, and have used with students. Most of the suggestions, if used with care, at the right time in a child's life, can be helpful and bring success to you and the child. Also, you may want to add other things to this collection of hints and advice from your own personal experience. Take notes if needed as you teach and guide others as to what works, when it works and why it works. After a while, you will have your own book.

Learning, no matter what age the person is, occurs in very similar ways. People never stop learning, so I've included information that may prove helpful to young adults, especially those just starting out on their own. Older adults may have no experience for one reason or another in some situations and in need of the information covered in this book also. There is no shame in that, so use this book to your advantage as a self-help book. Some of this information I give, I learned the hard way. Hopefully, it won't be so hard for you. Some children need help with starting to learn, or encouragement along the way, so maybe you can help. Keep in mind that not all people are the same and that one suggestion or method doesn't always work with everyone. So, the parent, teacher, guardian, friend, grandparent or concerned person should know that they need various learning tools and skills in order to help nudge a child on in the process of learning. Learn to adapt according to need, skill level and aptitude. This book is not intended to be a "Bible on Learning", so as you go along feel free to alter the suggestion into what works for you, the individual. Patience is a virtue in instruction as well as in learning, so don't give up. You will learn perhaps as much as the person you are trying to help in your interactions with one another. Count each step of progress as a success, be encouraged, keep learning, keep trying and keep on climbing!

Many thanks to all my students, and to all my teachers that I've had over the years. Sincerely,

MB

12/2024

1.
Starting at the Beginning

Advice for Parents of Young Children:

Start early, if you are the parent, start at least as early as the child can focus his or her attention. Identify things, sing, read rhymes, as well as children's stories to the baby. Make songs out of words, and sing words spelling the words out. Sound out clearly simple basic words. Hold up objects and name them, repeatedly, and have a show and tell time with them. Repetition is an important aspect of learning. Repetition shows importance to a young mind. Smile and be friendly as you go along. A reward can be as simple as a smile. Even with older people, never assume any level of knowledge or understanding without inquiry first. Always establish a starting point first, as to where to begin.

Toddlers

As a child grows older, get them fun, learning games and toys. Make and give them games that you can participate in with them. This will not only be educational, but it will help with what is called bonding. The child learns to trust the one who is with them, so that usually means their instructor. This is the principle of bonding: a familiar trust. That time with them, should preferably be a particular time period of the day. This will get them into a routine, and a regular schedule. Daily schedules are important, psychologically, and biologically. We see this in our usual routines of eating at certain times. In a similar way, the brain is like this also. The child will look forward to a good learning session if done correctly.

Basic Principles of Learning

Several suggestions in these sessions: to enhance thinking abilities (good advice for everyone)

1.Keep it Simple.

Never overwhelm the child, or yourself with information. The child will discard most of it and time will be wasted. Too much information complicates things. If it is you learning, take information in as if it were food, in bites. Keep feeding your brain, until the feast is over. Take time to digest what you have read. If there is too much presented all at once, it will not be totally remembered. So, it is best to start with foundational ideas that are mere skeletons of the entire concept. You can scan over a subject to get the general idea first. Do that with your explanations to your children or students.

2. Keep it logical.

Keeping it logical goes along with the keeping it simple idea. Simple sentence structures with no big words helps the child to think in sentences. Take a complicated concept or sentence and break it down into a simpler "in other words." Thinking in complete sentences is fundamental to logical thinking. As the child matures, insure that your child or student answers in complete sentences and not just short answers as in a word or two. If necessary, do not accept an answer unless it is presented in sentence form. Sentence form answers insure the thought processes was most complete. This should be done even in math. The student should be able to explain how the answer was obtained. The child must progress to paragraph making from their sentences. This shows the development of complete thoughts. Do not permit a child to jump from one topic to the next in rapid succession with incomplete sentences. Unless corrected, the child maybe sadly labelled "Scatter-Brained," later by their critics. Teach the child to organize their thought patterns and how to concentrate on one subject to completeness one at a time.

Most common logic involves only two main principles:

First Law is the Law of Non-Contradiction. This simply says that a statement for it to be logical cannot contradict itself. Inconsistencies are not logical. As an example: Planet X orbits beyond Pluto, but Planet X exists close to the sun. Here we see an impossibility in thought, and thus it is not logical.

The Second Law of Logic commonly used is the Law of Excluded Middle. This law of logic simply says that a statement must be either true or false with no middle ground. Logic is binary. It's either true or false. Sometimes in life we can't make up our minds as to whether something is true or false and categorize it as a "maybe." This does not negate the laws of logic. In such cases, our minds must sift the evidence for a proof one way or another as to whether something violates the laws of logic. A logical mind will come to a correct conclusion by examining the evidence of what is true and what is not true. Keep your sentences logical.

Only truth is the most logical. A liar is most often detected by inconsistencies. Truth in all fields of study is the foundation of knowledge Lies can be useful, however, though not fundamental to thought. A made up story of fiction is nothing but a drawn out lie with extensive detail, but can be used for entertainment as well as to teach certain lessons. Such drawn out lies that form stories must have logic supporting them to be enjoyable. Probably the most well known in this would be Aesop's Fables, or Fairy Tales by certain authors or traditions. A story, or sentence, without logic can only be a word salad and of little or no value at all. .Teach the children the value of telling the truth, once learned, it will go a long ways. Stay logical yourself, and be a good example to others.

Sometimes things can look to have elements of truth and falsehood in them. This is deceptive in the fact that all things must be either true or false, with no in between grey areas.. Quantum Physics verges on being not logical in some of its associated theories. One being the idea that something can indeed be in two places at the same time. This flies in the face of common logic and is best left up to the theorists. So, we should be teaching our children to think things out logically. Don't waste anyone's time learning and teaching things that are not true. It is one thing to get answers, but it is much better to get well thought out answers that are provable. Common sense is logical.

3. Keep Repeating as Needed:

It is best to repeat something or subject until it is fully grasped before going on to the next subject. As you see here, I keep repeating how important repeating is! Stick with a subject until mastered, unless time does not permit. Remember to reward each time, especially at success, no matter how small.

Math encourages logical thinking in that one must learn certain basic, foundational principles to begin with in order to progress. Thus, logically, recognition of numbers is taught first, then, counting. Next adding should be taught, then, multiplication. Of course the undoing of counting and adding is subtraction. The undoing of multiplication is division, so numbers are learned properly backwards and forwards. Patterns exist in numbers that can be easily seen in what is called multiplication tables. Such patterns once realized makes the study of numbers more logical to the student. A principle in math should be repeated, preferably in a different presentation, until it is fully grasped. One cannot successfully do a multiplication problem unless one can add correctly. Memorization is necessary to do multiplication easily. So, the child must retain the chart in their mind. A person can train the brain to remember by memorization. Word association helps prompt the memory. If kept active, even an elderly person can be brilliant.

Memory is where a person gathers information and stores it to be retrieved later. Usually, if there is little or no gathering, the person is not interested, not motivated, distracted, biologically incapable or inhibited. There also may be something wrong with the presentation. We can help motivate to learn in different ways. It is up to the teacher or adult to find the motivator and strike up interest in a young person. An adult must be self-motivated and prompted by certain goals viewed as valuable.

Reading

Words need to be understood by the letters and sounds first. Once a letter is recognized be sure the child is able to pronounce it with what it sounds like. Reading is fundamental to thinking. Reading a story helps the child think logically in sentences. Phonics is fundamental to being able to read. The instructor should obtain a good set of books on phonics and be sure that the child can sound the words out for themselves. Sight words, that is, words that are merely recognized upon sight from memory must be basic fundamental words that can be built upon. No one can be considered a highly skilled reader using only sight words. Both phonic skills and sight word vocabularies help to build good readers. Teach the child word vocabularies, but keep them at their level or a little above. Spelling goes with reading. Read to your child/student and have books on their level available. Visit a public library.

Rules for Spelling

1. Every syllable includes at least one vowel.
2. S never follows X, use a C after an X as in exercise.
3. I (i) comes before e except after C in most cases.
4. With very few exceptions, U (u) always follows Q (q).
5. If an s, f or an l fall at the end of a one syllable word, they are doubled, as in tall, stiff, kiss.
6. Plural words that end in s only have one s.

7. When adding a suffix that starts with a vowel to the end of a word that ends with a silent e, drop the e. as in bracing. The exception is when adding able as in manageable.
8. When adding a suffix to a word that ends in y, keep all the letters.
9. Prefixes usually don't change a word's spelling.
10. Almost no words in English end in either v or j.
11. Its without the apostrophe is possessive case (shows ownership).

It's with the apostrophe is a contraction for it has.

Rules of English Grammar

(Understanding the rules enhances understanding)

SENTENCES IN ENGLISH are usually made of two basic parts: the subject and the predicate. The subject is what the sentence is all about, and the predicate, usually following the subject in the sentence, is made of the verb (usually an action). The subject can be a noun or pronoun, and the predicate can be an action verb or a state of being verb.

A noun is either a person, place or thing, . Ex: man, woman, toy

A proper noun is the name of a particular person, place or thing. Ex: Jim, Helen, Barbie Doll

A pronoun is another word for a person, place of thing and takes the place of the noun, or proper noun, Ex: he, she, it.

An Adjective is a noun modifier, describing the noun. Ex: the big man. It usually comes before the noun that it describes.

Verbs can be either an action, " such as ran, jump," or a "state of being" verb: am, is, was, were,"

An Adverb is a verb modifier, describing the verb, and almost always ends in "ly" and mostly comes after the verb it modifies. . Ex: ran quickly

A predicate adjective is used in the predicate of a clause to describe either the subject of the clause or the direct object of a verb.

A Direct Object is the receiver of an action. EX: He threw the ball.

Prepositions: are words that show position: EX: to, from, under, around, over...He threw the ball over her head. The phrase following the preposition is usually called a prepositional phrase, as in "over her head."

Conjunctions: joiners of clauses, nouns or phrases

Coordinating conjunctions are used to join two or more words, phrases, or independent clauses that are grammatically equal or similar in both importance and structure. There are seven coordinating conjunctions in English, which can be remembered using the acronym FANBOYS: "for, and, nor, but, or, yet, so."

A comma must be used between two independent clauses. EX: "He ran, and she jumped." A comma must be used before a last item on a list. It is usually not thought proper to begin a sentence with a conjunction, but may be used to show continuation.

Subordinating conjunctions join a main, clause or complete thought to a clause that depends on the other clause for completeness of thought and clarity. EX: "as, because, since... John is going to the store since they were out of bread.

Subject verb agreement. A singular subject requires a singular verb. A plural subject requires a plural verb.

A plural noun usually ends in s. boys. Adding 's makes it possessive (shows ownership), boy's. Boys' is plural possessive.

A singular verb may end in s. was, is . The boy is... The boys are...

Hearing and Seeing:

Something else that is important, especially at the beginning, early stage. Be sure the child who is to learn can hear and see correctly. You can do an easy check of this yourself, and if in doubt, have the child checked out professionally. It is a sad thing to expect a child who is not able to see well to perhaps even focus on a page in front of them. It may be next to impossible for a child to learn to speak and thus read well if they have a hearing defiantly. Take the time to check for possible problems. A child who may not either see or hear well is at a definite disadvantage in the classroom.

Vaccines:

Along this line of health, this is rather controversial, but, I don't recommend getting multiple vaccines all at one time. Go ahead and get the vaccines but space them out so that they don't hit all at the same time. There have been some problems associated with getting too much at once for school admission. So, yes, get the vaccines, but try to space them out for the well-being of your child. Once injected, it can't be undone, so we just need to be careful not to overwhelm the young person all at once. Use your own good judgment and consult your physician.

2.
Using Analyzing (Helpful) Tools

ANALYTICAL (HELPFUL) tools can be of your own making and techniques, nothing "store bought."

Reading:

One can simply have the student or child sit in front of you to read. You hold the book up so that it is just below your eyes and watch them read out loud. Do their eyes wonder? Must they back track considerably? The answer to these questions will indicate attention level and concentration. Can they stay focused? If not there could be other problems. There could be some simple factors involved in the lack of concentration. Are they hungry? Instead of thinking about what they are supposed to read, they are concerned about their empty stomach. Are they tired? If so, why. Do they have sleeping problems? Are there at home problems? Another consideration is the question of their health. Are they sick? So, not all reading problems are consistently a lack of skill or education.

May have reading and book sharing times: Reading Clubs

Phonics Charts- Below are phonics sounds with associated words, that will help with sounding out words for the beginner.. You may feel free to make up your own individual charts with more illustrative words; it's not difficult. . The more words used for sounding out the better. Pictures also help with sounding and word association. Listen to how the child is pronouncing the sound back to you, and correct errors if possible.

Vowel Sounds- I will use the most commonly used words for this:

A a as in apple (sound familiar? This was probably how you were taught)

E, e as in egg

I, I as in I am

O, o as in on

U, u as in up

a_e, as in age

e_e as in these

i_e as in ripe

o_e as in bone

u_e as in rude.

Consonant Sounds-

b as in ball

c as in car, a "k" sound

c as in dance an "s" sound.

d as in dog

f as in fox

g as in go

g as in stop

h as in hand

j as in jump

k as in kite

l as in light

m as in man

n as in net

p as in pig

r as in run

s as in say

s as in raisin (z sound)

t as in toe

v as in van

w as in wind

x as in box

z as in zebra

Examples of Consonant Blends:

br as in break

cr as in crayon

dr as in drink

fr as in frog

gr as in grape

pr as in prune

tr as in truck

wr as in wrap

sc as in score

sk as in sky

sm as in small

sn as in snug

sp as in space

st as in stack

sw as in swing

If you buy phonics charts, many of them have associated pictures that are helpful. You may also completely do away with any sort of written chart of your own, but simply point to or pick up an object and sound it out. You can do this outside or while riding in the car. Have fun making a game of it! Supplement phonics with vocabulary words. Reading to the child is always important.

VISIBLE PROGRESS CHARTS:

The student or child has their name boldly on a chart. The chart can be public or the private property of the child. Once something is accomplished a star is put on the chart by their name. If it is public as in a classroom, one may have a system of rewards that go along with the chart. Such rewards could be line leader, door openers. Teacher's helper for the day, an earned exemption from a certain activity or test. Use your imagination. Children like contests and rewards, but be sure each level has its own rewards. One reward doesn't outshine another reward and may be used at different levels various times to level it out. What we don't want is that some of the slower students to get shamed by the 'star student group." So, each must be rewarded in their own way, and each recognized as being the best effort. It must be an encouraging thing or it will be detrimental. The idea of a chart will help analysis of motivation. What motivates certain children becomes evident. It is important to know this. Charts are only to be temporary along with certain contests. Variation of activity will demonstrate strengths and weaknesses, along with what motivates. So, use variety in this helpful tool.

Math Charts: memorization of the multiplication tables is of fundamental importance.

Math helpers.

These are children who simply help in the classroom with a pointer to the board, or writing a problem up for all to see. They don't have to be able to work the problem, but simply write on the board what is said, such as nine times eight equals. Then when someone in the classroom answers, they are the ones to write it down on the board. One must consider the student first. Some students are such that standing in front of the classroom for any reason would be a traumatic experience. So, before hand, be prepared and ask students who would like to be a math helper. Usually, there will be a good response. The one who never volunteers probably has reasons for not wanting to do so. At this point, depending on your skill level, you may want to see if the child would profit from being drawn out of the shell they are hiding in. School Psychologists that are available may prove to be helpful if it is decided that it is a good direction to go. Consultation with parents, along with the school administration, in this regard is to be considered fundamentally helpful. Establishing helpers for certain things, besides math, such as events and days is a good tool to observe student behavior, strengths and weaknesses.

A math helper also may be a student who has learned a process such as addition, multiplication etc. who will assist other students in showing them how the problems are worked. They can do this individually by going from student to student, or explaining it in their own words in front of the class. The goal is that each student should be able to explain how to solve the problems.

Individual Attention: a big help for everyone

Whether you are instructing a grandchild, or a classroom, individual, personal attention is a great tool. For this reason, most schools endeavor to limit the number of students per classroom. The student, no longer a baby, or toddler, also bonds this way. Personal attention show importance. During the time you spend with the individual learner, they may very well feel that they are at that moment, important. Suddenly, what is in front of them whether it is reading, math, history or science, that is for the moment instantly important. Be sure the time you spend with them, is focused. Once finished, you should be confident that your time together profited their understanding of the subject at hand. If working a math problem, they should be able to demonstrate that they can work the problems themselves, now, and know the reason it works that way. Be sure not to starve one student for the attention of another if possible. Some students are attention getters and thrive on the one on one relationships of classroom individual attention times. Use some judgment on this situation. If a student cannot grasp the principles in the allotted time, then, they probably need a tutor, which may or may not be you. You can learn much about a student using individual attention as a tool.

Computers and Audio-Visual Aids:

We need not overlook the great advantages we now have with the common usage of the computer, and cell phones with internet access. As a protective precaution, cell phones should be closely monitored by adults the younger the child is. Please do not just give a cell phone to a child and let them have full reign on it. Too many children are led astray and even disappear each year who fell victims to internet predators. This includes minors of all ages. Some schools use individual phones for educational purposes, especially at home studies.

Laptops, desktop computers, and smart phones can be valuable educational assets if used with discretion. Old fashioned films on a large screen in the front of the classroom can be useful. See your school resource advisor for suggestions on recommended programs if not dictated by the school curriculum. At home, parents may want to explore the educational programs that are offered on various channels such as PBS. One can download an educational segment for a particular lesson as desired. It is best to preview it, and have prepared questions to ask the student afterwards.

3.
Using Games and Activities

In this chapter we will describe several activities for students of various ages. It will be up to you to decide which ones are appropriate for the student or students you are dealing with.

Shoe box projects:

-Doll house with made furniture.

-Shoe box garden with real, small growing plants (box needs lined or have pots placed in it.

-Outdoor scene or ocean scene shoebox.

-Art display box

-Story, or Bible story shoe box, displays well known scene

-Environmental, habitat display shoebox

-Holiday shoebox

-Checker or Chess clubs- games and tournaments.- see our section on how to play Chess.

-Puppets

The easiest to make will be simply made from being cut out of cardboard and with straws used to manipulate the arms, legs and even mouth. Facial characteristics and clothing can be drawn and colored on or attached to the cut out cardboard figure. These puppets may be further used to put on classroom puppet plays. The teacher may have a puppet also to be used as a special guest in the classroom to teach. A sock puppet is easy to make also, but will require the sacrifice of someone's sock. A puppet will instantly get the students attention if age appropriate. Probably the fourth grade level would be the highest level for having a puppet assistant. Lower grades love puppets.

The highlight of a school year could possibly be the presentation of a puppet play where parents are invited to watch the program. Not only would interest be high and anticipated, but parents will have a chance to visit and observe their child in action. Some students may not have the chance to participate directly in operating a puppet, so these children may be greeters, door keepers and ushers, being sure everyone has a program. For such an activity, various kinds of puppets should be used. Some students who aren't puppet operators, can be the stage crew, raising and lowering the curtain, possibly playing the prerecorded theme music, and dimming the lights. The teacher should make sure to include each child in the classroom in some sort of role and make them feel like it's an important role. Mistakes will be made, but be sure that it is minimized the best it can be. Use all activities such as this, to encourage all in the right direction, and have fun doing it.

Where's Elmo (or equivalent)

Select a small toy, usually a human figure of some type. Hide the toy in plain sight, in different places every day before the first student arrives in the morning. Students must be in their seats and quiet to participate. Have a reward for the student who is observant enough to spot the small toy first. Creates excitement for showing up every day, and enhances observation.

Charades-

This is a fun acting game that requires minimal additional equipment. Even those who do not want to stand in front of the class and perform have the chance to participate. It may help to bring some children out of their shells and add excitement to the classroom. The teacher or adult may actually choose something or someone of particular interest for a given subject like reading or history. Some general ideas on charades:

1. Choose up teams or sides, this depends on the number of players. Minimum number per team is two.
2. Topic Cards- This can be hand written by the adult or typed words on small pieces of paper. Topics can be any pertinent subject. Usually the topics can be anything, from famous, or historic people, books, book characters, classroom items. And so on. Use your imagination, but don't get too distant. The slips of paper with the topics goes into a hat, or a bowl to be randomly chosen by the player.
3. Take Turns to be fair. Teams take turns with one team member acting out the charade chosen from the bowl or hat.
4. Timing- for this you can use a wall clock, or a watch. Each team has equal time, which is one to three minutes at most.
5. Actors-team members must communicate the idea word or phrase to their teammates without speaking, or mouthing the words, no singing aloud. Miming, gestures, and facial

expressions are the approved method of hints.
6. Guessing- the teammates guess at the answer before the time lapses
7. Scoring- the team must correctly guess the subject before time runs out in order to score a point.

Rules-

No words or sounds, no props just gestures- act it out.

Special Rule: an actor can skip a difficult subject at the loss of a point.

Winning the Game:

Each team is allowed a certain number of "rounds" or else when each player has had a turn. The team with the most points wins the game. This game can also have a maximum time limit, or round limit.

Spelling Bees-
This is a familiar activity that displays students spelling abilities. Those who drop out early should receive added attention in their skill building. This is an educational tool if used properly. Classrooms can be divided according to ability teams so that not just the very best spellers who are at the top of their class win. Words for each ability team should be adjusted to the expected skill level for the teams to enjoy some success. These could have team names and leagues. The spelling bees can be used on a regular basis, such as monthly, or just on occasions. There also can be school wide spelling bees if so desired.

Math Games-

Math games can be set up in similar manner as with other classroom games. They also can be used individually.

Speed Math-

Each student has a certain amount of time to finish a problem correctly to score a point. When the problem is solved the one who has scored the point explains how the problem is worked. Teams may be chosen with a mix of talents in each team. Try to pair opponents according to skill levels. You may play until the first team reaches a certain score or the activity may be timed. As with spelling bees, teams may be chosen according to abilities and leagues formed.

Math Baseball-

Teams will participate and may end with having a "World Series" with the two best teams. There are variations on how this game is played. Usually, simpler problems are base hits, and you may picture the players on the board or a large paper. Home runs are with harder, even complex problems presented to the player who is up to bat.. Strike outs are wrong answers which usually are just one wrong answer. If your answer is wrong, then, you have to go back to the end of the line up and wait your turn to be up again. Those who make hits can stand in order in the front of the classroom. You may place or draw a stick figure on the board to represent the player. If on a large display paper, cut-out figures may be moved around the bases. The team retires after three outs. You can have as many innings as you choose to have or as time permits.

Math Round Robin-

This is a game for the lower grades, up to fourth. A student will start on one side of the classroom and stand beside another student's desk. Math flash cards will be used for this activity, either number recognition, or simple addition or subtraction may be used. Whoever is fastest solving the problem gets to go on to the next person. The number of people passed should be recorded so that after all have had a chance to play, the best player will have the most people passed.

Jeopardy-

This is set up similar to the television game show. A box may be drawn on the board that has other boxes in it with dollar amounts. The teacher or adult will have the questions already prepared and in hand for the game. There are different categories for each column to be selected from: math, science, history, etc. The team of students may consist of their row, and rows will take turns playing, usually on certain days. Raised hands will suffice for notification of an answer, buzzers are not necessary. A score will be kept and once all the questions are answered, along with the "final round" a winner can be declared. Championship teams may compete at the end of the quarter, semester or end of the year. This is a good, general subject exercise.

Debates-

This activity is appropriate for upper grades, and can be interesting. Most often this falls into a social studies class activity. For this activity a topic of debate must be chosen by either the teacher or the students. Students need coached on how to carry on a proper debate. General rules and suggestions are as follows:

Things to keep in mind concerning debates:

There are 2 sides in a debate: Players must choose a side:

The affirmative (positive) side is in favor of the subject or topic

The negative side rejects the acceptance of the subject or topic.

The Team Line is a basic statement that is presented by the first speaker of a team supporting the subject of debate as true and good. Each team is to have a "team line" which should be short and referred to by the other team members. The negative team has a negative line that is used to contradict and oppose the positive team's line. A debate team is to have three members.

Debate Announcer and Time Keeper:

The debate announcer announces the topic as well as introduces the teams and their players to the audience.

The debate announcer announces the rules of the debate.

Each team member will be timed with a minimum of three minutes

The time keeper will tap the desk when the three minutes are up.

Each team has equal time.

> The debate speakers will speak in a certain order.

> The first speaker of the affirmative position must do the following:

> Define the subject

> Present the team's line

> Outline what each of the team members will speak about

> Finally, present the first half of their position.

> The First Speaker of the negative position is to:

> Accept or reject the affirmatives definition. If this isn't done then automatically it is assumed that the negative side agrees with the positive definition.

> Present the team's line

Speakers:

First Speaker of the Negative Side Must

- accept or reject the definition. If you don't do this it is assumed that you accept the definition.
- present the Negative team's line.
- Outline what each team speaker will cover.
- Refute several of the main points of the opposing team.
- The first team speaker should spend approximately one fourth of the team's time refuting the other side.
- The first team member is to present the first have of team's argument.
- Next: the Second Affirmative team member is to
- Reaffirm the team's line
- Refute the main points given by the first negative speaker
- Should spend about one third of their time refuting the other team.
- Present the second half of the affirmatives position.
- The second negative speaker is to:
- Reaffirm the team's line
- Refute some main points of the opposing team not already covered
- Spend about one third of the time refuting the opposition.
- Present the second half of the negative side's position.

The Third affirmative speaker is to

Reaffirm the team's line

Rebut the any remaining points of the negative's side or those that haven't been dealt with sufficiently.

Spend about three fourth's of available time in rebuttal.

Summarize the team's position with a conclusion

The Third Negative team member is to

Reaffirm the team's line

Rebut all outstanding points of the opposition.

Spend about three fourth of the allotted time in rebuttal.

Summarize the team's position, and draw to a conclusion.

No third team member, either the affirmative or negative may introduce any new concepts or evidence that have not already been introduced during the debate.

Rebuttal simply means criticizing. There is to be no name calling or profanity.

All rebuttals must show why the other side is wrong. Usually the most common way of doing this is to show the other sides position to either not make sense, contradictory, self-defeating and or detrimental to all parties involved.

Rebut the main points as given by the opposition. Do not set up a strawman rebuttal in a debate. A strawman is a logical fallacy that involves a misrepresentation of an opponent's position.

Do not criticize a speaker personally, criticize their words and positions.

Shouting and noise making are inappropriate in any debate format.

The use of "cue cards" is acceptable in debates.

Make sure you speak loud enough for all to hear, as well as speak clearly.

Be polite and well mannered, it will gain the respect of everyone.

Crafts:

Crafts are great for educational interaction. Please, select crafts of interest, and viable in the classroom or home situation. It is always a great idea to find a parent that enjoys a craft who is willing to share it with the classroom. Ask your students if any of their parents do crafts or hobbies who would be willing to share with the class. Such activities may include knitting, crocheting, watercolor painting, drawing, coloring, charcoal paints. Mask making in paper-mache, decorated fan making, colored paper flower making. The list is endless and only limited by your imagination, resources and time. .

The class can be divided up during craft time into the interested groups with parents giving the instruction for each group. Some parents will only be willing to do a one time craft session, but others will volunteer as so desired. Don't forget to tell the parent your appreciation for their time and effort.

How to make paper-mache-

Supplies for the project: newspapers, paste, mixing bowl, a form to mold the paper-mache into given shape.water, water color paint.

No-cook paste requires only all-purpose flour, water, a bowl and a whisk It's one part water to two parts flour. While mixing, it should be thin, and runny, if not, it's too thick. Mix until there's no lumps. Paste is ready to be used. Projects can be bowls, face masks, pinata's, globes using balloons, planets and a model of the solar system, and of course one of the favorites, a volcano.

How to make a paper-mache volcano:

Mold the Volcano:

Form the volcano by crumpling newspaper around the sides of the selected cup (can use bottle for larger volcano) into cone shape. Now, wrap the cone with masking tape.

Form the Volcano

Start to build the form of the volcano by wrapping crumpled newspaper around the sides of the bottle or cup, making it as wide as you want at the bottom. Mold and shape it into a cone so the volcano is narrower at the top of your bottle or cup than it is at the base.

1. Wrap the volcano cone in Masking Tape smoothly to give strength to the shape.
2. Add layers of newspaper strips with paste to get the cone the size desired.
3. Allow to dry about a day.
4. Paint the volcano as desired adding detail.
5. Lava:

One tablespoon of warm water goes into the volcano top. Add four drops of dishwashing detergent, next add some baking soda and stir. For color a few drops of food coloring of the desired color (usually red ore yellow). For the explosion, pour vinegar into the volcano top. Warning: do not stand over the volcano or close to it after the vinegar is added.

Small Projects:

One must not forget the value of the small, quick project for easy, rapid success. Small quick projects that only take up a short period of time can be encouraging as well as rewarding. Below is a short list of a few. Use your imagination to vary these suggestions:

1. Paper cut-out snow flakes

2. Milk or juice carton bird houses
3. Stick airplanes made from a clothes pin for the body, and "craft sticks" (looks like tongue depressors) glued on by school glue for the wings.
4. Paper flowers
5. Book covers
6. Paper pinwheel
7. Sock puppets

Snow flakes-

You need to have a square sheet of paper, usually white. Square means all the sides are of the same length (same size). Typing paper cut to size is a common choice. Fold the paper diagonally so that it forms a triangle. Open the paper back up and fold the other half to make a triangle in it also.

Cut the folded edge with triangular cut outs. Cut along the outside edges as well as make different shaped cutouts in the body of the snowflake. Unfold and examine work. You may want to refold and add cuts or add color to your creation.

Milk Carton Bird Houses-

1.clean milk carton

2. spray paint carton desired color and allow to dry.

3. cut out the door with a utility knife a few inches from the bottom. Keep in mind the size of a bird so you don't want it too large or too small.

4. Decorate if desired. Remember, paint takes time to dry, so don't get in a hurry with tthis.

5. a perch- insert a select stick into a hole about an inch below the door, and secure it with glue, hot glue works best.

6. Drain holes need poked into the bottom for water drainage.

7. Cut a hole on both sides at the top of the carton to be able to hang it. Run a strong string not subject to rot from moisture through the top.

8. Optional: spray a clear sealant over the outside to your birdhouse to make sure it doesn't fall apart before the bird is done using it. Usually the carton can be expected to last the season without it because it comes with a waxed surface.

9. Hang the bird house within view of one of your windows. This may require embedding a pole in the ground if no trees are available. Some communities have rules as to what can be in yards.

Paper Flowers- Daisies.

You will need paper the desired colors of your flower. A daisy for instance will require green, white and yellow paper. Two strips of yellow paper eight to ten inches long, approximately two inches wide, four white pieces of paper about four to six inches square, two green pieces: one being three inches by four, the other three inches by six.

Fold the yellow strip length wise once, then cut the strip in half and refold

Cut the folded strip on one edge approximately one half to three fourths deep all along that one edge.

Take the square, white piece of paper and fold it diagonally, three times. Next cut the white folded sheet into elongated ovals for the pedals of the flowers. Unfold the pedals and they should all be joined at one circular end. If not you have cut too much. Take your fingers and bend the pedals so that they don't lie flat but have upward curves to each pedal. Do this with all four white pieces of paper to make a full flower.

Take your green paper and fold it lengthwise twice, then cut triangular notches off the one long side and unfold. The other green piece of paper cut into the shape of a long pointed leaf.

Take your yellow strips that have been leaf cut on one edge and run a line of school glue down the uncut edge. Next, lay a green pipe cleaner down on the one end of the yellow paper with the stem sticking out away from the uncut side. Turn the yellow around the end of the pipe cleaner tightly until it is totally wrapped around the end of the pipe cleaner. Do this same thing with the second yellow slip of paper, placing it over the other one with the cut edges facing the same direction. Be sure to use adequate glue especially at the end of the paper to secure it.

Next place the white pedals on top of each other and poke a hole through the center of them. Put glue n the center of each one and space the pedals out so that they fan out and are not on top of each other.

Put glue at the base of the yellow paper where the green stem comes out so that the white pedals will stick there. Push the bottom of the green stem through the center holes of the flower pedals so that they come to rest at the base of the yellow paper. Next carefully spread the yellow paper out so that it has the appearance of the center of a daisy. Glue the leaves on and allow to dry.

Physical Activities-

People of all ages need activity and this should not be ignored. A child's education that includes physical activities of various games promotes mental as well as physical health.

Suggested Activities (consider age, abilities and environmental surroundings in any selection).

Tag

Hide-n-Seek

Kick Ball

Baseball or Softball

Basketball

Field Hockey

Soccer

Tennis

Outdoor Lunches

Nature Walks

Relay Races

Field Trips

Hopscotch

Volleyball

Toy Car Races

Frisbee

Most of these activities need little or no explanation, but all should have supervision by at least one adult.

-Simple Rules of Baseball- (similar rules are used for most games that involve base running)

Two teams will oppose each other in the game. Regular baseball has nine players in a team, but in children's sports this can vary as in a seven member team.

The game is made up in nine innings, giving each team time at bat, and the other plays the field.

Scoring a run (a point) involves a team player hitting the ball and being able to advance either their selves or other team members around the bases to come across home plate (where the ball is batted)

The team with the most runs at the end of the nine innings is the winner..

The game can have a time limit instead of a set number of innings. There can be less number of innings, also usually seven or five.

Outs-: if a batter swings and misses at a pitched ball three times their turn is over and is called "out"

A ball player can be tagged out by an opposing player who has the ball while in play.

A ball player is out if they hit a ball and it's caught in the air. It must not touch the ground.

Player Positions: batter- the player who's turn it is to bat the ball. I goes in a designated order. Pick a bat to match the player. Bats come in different lengths and weights.

Field Positions- Catcher-one who crouches at the home plate and catches the pitched ball for the field team.

Pitcher- person who stands on a pitcher's mound or designated area and pitches (throws) the ball to the catcher at home plate. The batter tries to bat the ball so as to not be caught by the catcher, or any field player. In soft ball, the pitch must be underhanded.

Base players- Field players must have a person at each base so that they will be able to catch the ball and hold it before a runner from the opposing team is able to run to that base.

Umpire- person not favoring either team and is an objective observer of the action. This person calls the pitched balls as either strike (worthy) or a ball (not hittable in the batter's square or immediate area in front to the batter- no higher than the shoulder or lower than mid-thigh. The umpire also calls the decision as to whether a player from the batting team has made it to home plate before the ball is caught by the catcher, while in play.

Stealing a base- a player may advance to the next base while the ball is in play so long as they make it to the base before the ball does.

Basketball-

Each team is to only have five players on the court.

The court consists of a flat playing area with a basket ten feet off the surface.

A full court has two baskets one on each side of the court.

Each team is assigned a basket as their basket. This swaps at half-time. A score of two points occurs when a team is able to throw the basketball up so that it goes down through the basketball hoop of the opposing team.

The game begins when the two team's center players must jump for the ball in center court when tossed up by the referee. A ball teams center is usually the tallest person on the team for this reason

Team positions-

-Center- plays offensively and defensively.

Offensively this person gets open for passes, shoots and helps "screen" defenders. This player does the offensive rebounding and "put-backs"

Defensively is player is to block shots and passes from the opposing team and secures rebounds.

-Forward- second tallest on team and is positioned near the basket and by the wings or sides close to the opponent's basket.

Offensively- this player gets free (away from opposing team player) for passes, takes outside shots, drives for goals and does rebounds.

Defensively- Helps prevent opposing drives and gains the basketball in rebounds.

-Guard- usually the shortest player who has skills in dribbling and passing

Offensively- sets up plays, drives to the basket and shoots from long range.

Defensively- contests shots of the opponent with the ball, steals away passes from opposing team, helps prevent drives to the hoop by the opposition.

-Power Forward- position close to the oppositions basket, to the left of it, job is similar to Forward.

-Small Forward- position further away from opposing team's basket, close to center right.

-Point Guard- person who is closest to own team's basket, prevents being scored upon.

Fouls- are violations to the rules of play

-Charging- a player runs over a defensive player

-slapping, hitting, holding, pushing,

-Blocking- illegal contact by defender.

-Intentional Foul- this is contact made while presenting no intent to play the ball.

-Technical Foul- non-contact foul such as improper game conduct and un-sportman like behavior.

Violations-

Carrying the ball

Traveling- taking more than one and a half steps without dribbling.

Double Dribble- dribbling with both hands.

Held ball- two players gain possession of the ball at the same time. The referee stops play and awards the ball to one of the teams

Goaltending- an opponent attempts to interfere with the ball on it's way down through the net.

- Field Hockey-

Players must use the flat face of their playing sticks to hit and move the ball (dribble). They attempt to knock the ball past the goalkeeper and into the opponent's goal. The ball can not be kicked, held carried down field. Only shots taken within the "striking circle" count as a score. Goalkeepers can only play the ball with their stick once outside the circle. Field hockey has no "off-sides" as in football and some other field games. Hitting others with the stick is not permitted.

Soccer- (ie football)-

This game is to be played in a large field, basically, one hundred yards by fifty yards. Smaller fields are permitted for smaller players.

There is a circle ten yards in diameter in the center of the field.

Two goals with nets are set up at opposite ends of the field

A soccer team must have at least seven players, and at most eleven, with five substitutes.

For protection shin guards and helmets should be worn. Since running and rapid movement such as turns is required in the play of the game proper shoes with cleats should be worn.

Generally the game lasts ninety minutes with halves of forty-five minutes.

The referee does a coin toss at the beginning of the game to determine who does the initial kick-off to the other team.

A score occurs when the ball passes completely under the cross bar and between the uprights of the goal.

-American Football-

The game starts with a coin toss to see who will kick the ball off to the other team.

Games last for four fifteen minute sessions called quarters. There is a two minute break between quarters except the one between the second and third quarter. This is called half time and is fifteen minutes in length.

Each team is given four chances called downs to gain at least ten yards. This is done by running the ball, or throwing the ball to a receiver. After the required yardage is made, the down starts over again and the team has four more chances to gain yards. If the yardage is not made, then the team must give up the ball where it stands. This is called a turnover.

A path for a runner or receiver is called a route. Either the coach or the quarter back calls the play. The defensive captain calls the plays for the defensive team.

On a fourth down the offensive team has the choice of either playing the ball or punting it away to the other team. Often, if the offensive team is within the forty yard line of the opposition a field goal is attempted. Sometimes the offensive team will pretend to set up for a field goal but instead at the last few seconds, change the plan and either pass the ball or run it.

Six points is scored for a team successfully crossing into the opponent's end zone with the ball. After the six points the team can kick for an extra point.

-Tennis- (My Favorite)

-A two player game is called a singles match. A four player game is called a doubles. The players use a tennis racquet to hit the tennis ball back and forth over the net.

The ball must be hit so that it lands in the boundaries of the marked court for the play to continue, if not, the player who hit the ball out of bounds loses a point.

A point begins with the serve, which is when the "server" hits the ball from behind the baseline on their side into the opposite side service box.

A serve that fails to land in the opposite side service box or if the ball hits the net a fault results. Two faults in a row is called a double fault which takes a point away from that player.

The player or team wins by scoring four points, with a minimum two point margin.

Tennis Terms and Scoring:

A game is won when a player scores four points

A set is a group or collection of games that is played until someone wins six or more games.

A Q match is the best of either three or five sets.

A game is considered over when the first player scores four or more points: 15, 30, 40 and the game winning point.

Occasionally, both players score forty points, in which case it is called a "deuce". After that a player has to win two points in a row. The first point, is known as the "advantage," and then the game winning point. If the opponent wins the next point then it is a second deuce.

Scores:

0 points is called "Love"

1 point equals 15

2 points equals 30

3 points equals 40

Tied Score is called "All"

Server wins the deuce point it's called "Ad-In"

Receivers wins deuce point it's called "Ad-Out"

To win a set a player must win at least six games, with the stipulation that that player wins two games ahead. Example: if a game is 6-5, then the leading player has to win a seventh game to win the set.

In a tie-break game, (6-6), in which the scoring changes to simply 1, 2,3,up to seven. The first player to get to seven points with a lead of two points wins.

-Volleyball-

Winning a game of volleyball means you score more points than the opponent in the best of three or five sets.

Each team has equal number of players, usually six. Teams may have substitute players.

Each team may hit the ball up to three times to get it over the net. The defensive team tries to hit it back over the net without it hitting the ground. Only three tries is permitted.

Games can be played up to twenty-five points or an agreed upon number, but must be won with a two point lead.

A point is scored when a team successfully hits the ball over the net and it hits the opponent's ground.

A Rule Violation Occurs when:

Stepping over the base line while serving.

The ball hits the net and fails to go over. No violation occurs if the ball hits the net and still goes over.

A player holds, palms, carries, or runs with the ball.

A player touches the net, but is okay if accidental.

The ball travels under the net.

A player cannot reach over the net and hit the ball.

-Pickleball- (can be fast passed)

A coin toss determines who serves

This game is played on a badminton like court with the net in the middle. Pickleball paddles are made of wood or hard plastic. The ball is similar to a plastic wiffleball. Two or four players are permitted per game. Only the side that serves can score. Ball is served underhand. The ball must clear the net. The receiver side must let the ball bounce once before attempting to return the ball.

Ways a serving team can score:

Opponent volleys in a non-volley area or zone

The opponent fails to return the ball

The opponent knocks the ball out of the boundary limits.

To Win: the first side to score eleven points with a lead of two points. The play continues until a two point lead is obtained thereafter.

Indoor play:

-Chess- Rules and the Play.

A chessboard is a square board sectioned off into sixty-four squares, that make the design eight by eight. The squares are either black or white, and alternate so that there are no two white or two black squares sitting side by side. The horizontal rows going across the board are called ranks, and the vertical columns flowing away from the players are called files.

The two players have sixteen pieces, one king, one queen, two rooks, two bishops, two knights and eight pawns.

The larger pieces go on the closest rank to the player, and the pawns goes on the second rank as follows: The Queen goes on the central square of the same color that she is. A black queen goes on the black center square. The white queen goes on the white center square. Rooks usually pictured as an elephant are placed on the outside, right and left, corners. Knights usually pictured as a horse or a man on a horse sits immediately beside the rooks. The bishops, usually pictured as a cleric with a pointed hat, goes in the squares beside the knights working our way inward. The king is placed in the last empty square beside the queen.

Playing the game:

White goes first, often one is offered to pick the piece from a closed fist after being hidden behind the back. What ever color the piece is that is in the hand that is picked is the color that must be played. White has the first move. One cn not skip a move, even when making a move will cost the player a piece or two. The play will continue until the king is in checkmate, or there is a declared draw or one of the players resigns. If the play is being timed, and a player exceeds the time limit to move, unless that player can checkmate the opponent in that move, the game is lost by that player.

The different types of pieces dictate different patterns of movement.

All pieces move to an empty square unless capturing an opponent's piece. Except for the knight and for what is called castling (which can occur only once per player) between the rook and the king, pieces do not jump over any other piece on the board.

A piece is captured when an attacking piece actually lands on its square. A captured piece is then removed from the board and placed along beside the board along with other fellow captured pieces of like color. All pieces except the king can be captured and removed from the board. The king can be checked or checkmated numberous ways.

<u>The King</u> can move in any direction but only one square at a time except castling. Castling is when the king, still unmoved and sitting in its original square, is moved toward the closest rook, which is still sitting in its original square. The rook is moved from its original square to two spaces directly on the other side to the newly placed king. There must not be any pieces between the king and the rook. The king may not be under attack at the time of the move, nor is he permitted to move into a square that is under attack.

<u>The Queen-</u> a very powerful piece that can move vertically, horizontally or diagonally, but only in one direction per move. May move as many spaces as needed including across the board, but not jump pieces.

<u>The Bishop-</u> can move only diagonally, with unlimited number of squares, but not permitted to jump pieces. A bishop stays on its original color. A bishop that starts out on a white square must travel and capture on white squares The same is true of the black bishops.

The Knight- moves by jumping two spaces and then one to either the right or the left. It can jump over pieces. This is in the form of an L pattern.

The Rook- moves in an unlimited number of squares, either horizontally or vertically, but can't jump over pieces.

Pawns- A Pawn can move either one or two spaces forward on its first move, and only one space after that. It can move diagonally only to capture a opposing piece that sits immediately diagonal to it in a move called "en passant". Pawns do not move backwards. If a pawn manages to go across the entire board and into the last row (rank) of the opposition or (king's row)-the eighth rank, it may be promoted usually to a queen. A king can have more than one queen. Having two or more queens increases that sides power and may be overwhelming bringing the game to a quick end

Putting the King in check. The king is in check when under attack by at least one enemy piece. No other piece may be moved except to alleviate the attack. A piece may be moved between the king and it's attacker. A king may move aside to avoid the line of attack. A piece that comes between the king and an attacker, may not be able to move so long as the king remains in the same position and the attack continues. This is called being "pinned." One may not move a piece that will endanger the king. The king may also capture a piece if it sits next to it and the move doesn't place the king under new attack.

Checkmate- If a king cannot move out of being checked, it is said to be checkmated.

A player can quit the game at any time, or forfeit the game.

Stalemate or draw- The player cannot move the king, which presently isn't in check, if the only move that can be made will place it in the path of an attack.

You can have classroom tournaments. I've played multiple players for a challenge just to see how students were progressing. You may end up with several champions by the end of the year.

-Making up your own word puzzles-

1. Select words for your puzzle on child's level, can be spelling words.
2. Make an appropriately sized grid
3. Put the words inside the grid boxes.
4. Put in "filler" letters where needed
5. Test out your puzzle and make copies for the students.

This can be done in Microsoft Word or just about any word processing program. Crossword and word search puzzles will help children think about the word, its spelling and meaning. Some spelling books already have puzzles but if not, make your own as a helpful learning tool.

Do-It-Yourself Educational Projects

HERE'S A SHORT LIST of some possible simple projects:

1. A Terrarium in a Bottle
2. Home-made Solar Cooker
3. Static Levitation

4. Making Slime

5. Pop Rockets, Balloon Rockets

6. Water Filtration System

7. Water Cycle Models

8. Sun Dial

9. Water Erosion Model

10. Ant Farm

The possibilities are endless, so use your imagination. Keep it basic and keep it simple. Good Luck.

4.
Learning Responsibility

Teaching responsibility to children initially falls upon the parents. Good teachers also know the importance of responsibility and have learned to include it in their student's education. Without responsibility society becomes nonproductive, lawless and breaks down. We all have responsibility to one another as adults to be decent citizens of society. This must be instilled in the student in order to graduate productive good citizens of our nation. Sadly, modern education has adopted as its guiding golden rule that irresponsibility and failure have little or no consequences. Consequences enforce responsibility and good citizenship. A nation falls when it does not enforce its own laws to protect its own citizens.

Before we begin with more detail, it must be emphasized that we teach by example. A parent loses status in the sight of a child when they don't live up to their own words or expectations. The "Don't do as I do, do as I say," really isn't very effective in the long term. Besides being a good example to the learner, one must use positive reinforcement, and only negative reinforcement if absolutely necessary.

Being a good example means that we demonstrate how something is done or handled correctly. This means going beyond mere words. It also means that what is taught is to demonstrate value to the learner. Students are not interested in anything that appears to be a waste of time.

Responsibility also has its own rewards. A young person will learn the satisfaction of a job well done and will gain both confidence and pride. The teacher or parent should recognize the child's accomplishment and use some praise or even a reward if that is deemed necessary or has been promised. Never renege on a promise if at all possible. This is a way to break a child's trust if the adult has lied and will not follow through with that which has been stipulated to be the result of completion.

Thus clear expectations should be laid out at the beginning, along with any rewards or punishments. If the task is not very important and only minimal, then a reward or punishment may be skipped, though not verbally. Always check on the completion. One should encourage the child to do better, or at least try the next time. If the small task ended in failure, then, encourage to try to do better the next time. Point out the path to success, because it may not be clearly understood by a young person.

Use assignments in responsibilities as a growing thing. In other words, start small and simple, and then progress as the child increases in abilities and confidence. Some simple tasks to teach responsibility may include: making one's own bed, bathing self, dressing self, cleaning one's own bedroom, helping in the kitchen, help with yardwork, gardening, washing the family car, doing homework from school.

Rewards can be many and varied such as permission to play certain games, having friends over, permitting to visit a friend, candy, ice cream, a day off from responsibility, special trips somewhere, going to a game park, money, new clothes. If you choose to use rewards, be sure that the reward is a desired one by the child in question. Lack of motivation may be the result of choosing the wrong reward.

Negative things that could happen, if the responsibility is not successfully completed by the child, would be the temporary restriction of any of the above items of enjoyment. The child is to understand that you still love them as a parent even though they have not come up to expectations.

A teacher may find it necessary to have a parent teacher conference either at school or at the child's home if there are really bad infractions in behavior or performance. Visitation at the home may reveal certain problems that the teacher was not previously aware of, and may be factors in the failure of the student thus far. Serious problems ,such as home violence, should be turned over to the school administration and not handled by the teacher alone. The well-being of an innocent child is paramount for a school administration.

Ultimately, when adulthood is finally reached, a child who has been properly educated will be one that is competent to handle life's situations. For this reason, practical skills should be learned either at home or at school. We will briefly go over these in a later chapter with the title of practical skills. These are to be differentiated from academic skills such as in the sciences, history, and advanced forms of mathematics such as algebra, trigonometry, and calculus. Quite often, one can go through their entire lives and never have to use any one of these. This is not to say that they are not important, since as a youth, the future ahead is not certain. It is unknown if they will ever need these mathematical skills or not. College is not for everyone, and if not, then learning a post high school graduation skill will enhance a young adult's potential.

In this case, vocational education is a valuable addition to a person's learned abilities. One must be a high school graduate to get into most vocational schools, but there are exceptions. The potential student must consider three important factors: personal interests, personal skills, potential employment. One does not want to learn a skill to which there are no jobs. One must look at the demand of certain skills for this form of education to be practical. Being gainfully employed is a good reward for a person who has taken up the responsibility of having a planned future. Planning a future, step by step is a plan for having a successful life. It is best to stay in your skill level and be a success at that level before trying to go up the ladder. IAs the saying goes, "Failing to Plan, is Planning to Fail."

Growing up as a responsible person will help to eliminate failure in later life. Having a pet is a good way to teach responsibility. Have the child act as the owner, being in charge of the feeding, cleaning, and the animals exercise. This all depends on the maturity of the child. For this a small dog or cat works out best. Have the child accompany the pet to the veterinarian. This will help the child understand the value of getting shots, and taking care of one's health.

5.
Practical Skills for Older Children.

There are several necessary skills that every adult should have at least a minimum level of competency at achieving: Balancing a Budget; Car Maintenance; Cooking, Maintenance of a House, Maintenance of a Relationship. We will deal with these topics in an easy, straightforward way, sticking to the basics. These skills are important in adult life so they need to be covered before adulthood arrives for the sake of the child.

Making a Bed

Judging from what the typical teenager's bedroom looks like, they don't really know how to make a bed. Part of the problem is motivation. As a parent it is up to you to find the right motivational tool for this. At the teenager level, usually offering to grant some special request of theirs will work, but use your own good judgment. The key to this is to train them to make their beds daily as young children, so that when the rebellious teenage years come around, it will be something engrained into their daily habits. If you have to start from scratch for some reason, here are the usual steps for making a bed. Please be sure that the bedding is cleaned regularly. Sheets and blankets with a nice freshly cleaned scent, done at least once a week are the most desirable.

Check to see if the bed has what is called a "bed skirt." This looks like a sheet of cloth that extends down from the mattress to almost the floor. It serves as a decorative device to block the view to under the bed. It hides shoes, slippers and whatever you want to hide under the bed. If the bed skirt is lop-sided with one side longer than the other, one side touching the floor and the other side barely visible, then you will need to lift the mattress and pull it so that all sides look the same. Please remember to wash the bed skirt when you wash the rest of the sheets.

Some mattresses have an additional topper or pad that adds softness. These are held in place by stretchy straps in each corner. These also need washing on a regular basis.

If you don't have one, you may want to consider getting a mattress protector, which would go on next if you have one. It helps protect the mattress. Most mattresses have at least a ten year warranty, and if you should ever want to turn it in for warranty due to faulty springs or sections being sunken, the manufacturer will not take a dirty mattress, or one that is stained. The protector keeps it clean.

The sheet for the mattress comes next. If it is a flat sheet, not fitted, you will need to see which is the long side and short side so it will cover the mattress correctly. The same is true if it is a fitted sheet that has elastic corners. Once you determine which is the top and bottom of the sheet, start in one corner and tuck it under the mattress. A fitted sheet will help hold it in place. Then, go to the opposite side and tuck that side in. After you have tucked all four corners in, be sure the sheet is pulled tight so that there's no wrinkles in it.

The top sheet goes on next. Usually a top sheet will have a sewn doubled over section maybe two inches wide to designate the side that goes at the head of the bed. Lay this sheet out flat, and be sure it is equal on all sides, then tuck it in but leave the top, at the head of the bed, untucked so that it can be left pulled back revealing the pillows. An optional "hospital corner tuck" is where the tucks at each corner have a triangular shape.

The placement of blankets and comforters all follow the same pattern of being laid out smoothly and equally on all sides. Extra pillows and throw blankets may be added if desired.

Laundry

Everyone should know how to do their own laundry, so we will give a few tips for this subject.

First sort clothing, inspect for stains. Keep whites separate. New clothing that has never been washed need washed by themselves. New clothes coloring will come off on your other clothes if washed together. New clothes also should be washed in cold water.

Add stain remover directly to the stain. Usually, this is a spray. Spray the stain on both sides of the garment. Then take the garment in both hands and vigorously rub the spray into the stained fabric. For best results, leave the garment to rest a while afterwards.

If there is a baby involved, their clothes are sorted separately and mild detergent soap is used. Regular detergent may give a baby a rash.

If the garment has special washing instructions it should be posted on a tag up around the neck area. Some clothing requires "dry cleaning." You may want to add a fabric softener to the wash which usually leaves it with a desirable smell.

After the washing machine is done, inspect each article of clothing for cleanliness. If a stain is not completely out, re-apply the stain remover, or use something else, then rewash it, or save it for the next wash. If you throw the article of clothing into the dryer as is, with the stain still on it, the dryer will bake the stain into the garment forever. Be advised, some detergents are better at removing stains than others. Read the information on its container before purchasing. You also may want to use a "laundry sheet" to go into the dryer with your wet clothing. Those can remove such things as lint and animal fur, besides giving the finished laundry a desirable smell. It is best if you fold your clothes and/or hang them on hangers as you pull them from the dryer to prevent wrinkles. This also organizes your laundry so that it is ready to be put away.

-Balancing a Budget.

Having a bank account will help immensely. You can use automatic deductions to automatically pay your bills if you want. The bank will keep tabs on your running account, that you can check over the phone or computer as often as you like.

We will just start out by saying that what you make in income should be written in a book, preferably a ledger. If that is not available for some reason you may simply use a regular sized notebook with pages the size of typing paper to make your own. To do this draw vertical lines and form columns on the first page of your balance sheet in your financial journal. Date it at the top, usually by month, even if you get paid weekly or daily. If you are doing this yourself, five columns will usually work for most budgets On right side, the first line of the fifth column write the amount of money you have available to pay bills. On the left hand side column, second line, write the account that is owed. The next column write the account number down. The third column write the amount owed. The fourth column write the amount paid. You may want to annotate the date paid also here in small writing. The fifth column is the balance, or in other words the difference between the amount of money listed at the top for paying bills and the amount of the bill subtracted from it. This will give you a running total in the fifth column.

` The next bill to be paid will be listed on the third line, the third bill to be paid will appear on the fourth line and so on. This will work for paying most credit bills once a month. If it is a weekly payment, then a different leger page will need set up for that weekly account using the same basic tracking, except you will simply do a running total down the page as the bill gets paid. The total due will appear at the top and as the weeks go by the amount paid will be seen going down the page until it is finally paid in full. This may take months or years so other pages may be needed.

Check Books- are miniature account journals. One will need to keep track of the amount in the bank by accurately subtracting out what each check is made out for.

Credit cards- the word "credit" in accounting means what is owed so a credit card is a debt card. It is a negative not a positive. Basically with credit cards a bank will agree to what amounts to a uninsured loan. It is uninsured in that the borrower doesn't have to put up any collateral to gain the loan. The borrower has to simply agree with a signature to pay back the loan. Banks do this because of the high interest rates that are charged rewards them with lucrative income each month. In addition to the high interest rates charged there will be a monthly fee added to the bill, and then of course a substantial late fee if the minimum due isn't paid by the date due. The minimum fee due only covers the interest on the loan or only part of it in some cases. If the minimum due is only ever paid, the bill may take up to thirty years to finally be paid off if then. Every year, thousands of people find themselves overwhelmed by their creditors and must file bankruptcy. Unable to pay means all that has been purchased with the card may actually be expected to be returned, and if that isn't possible, personal assets may be legally required of the borrower to be turned over to the creditors. Historically, people have lost their homes and automobiles because of bankruptcy. Credit cards can be a huge burden if not kept under tight control.

Learn how to space out your expenditures according to your budget. You don't want all of your bills due on one week and you are broke until the next pay, so space them out, hopefully evenly. Also food and gasoline usage needs to be carefully controlled. You don't want to burn up all of your gasoline in your car with non-essential driving trips. Combine trips if you can so you are not on the road so much. It costs just to start an engine. Also, the same idea applies to food. You shouldn't buy groceries on one day, and binge eat so that the rest of the week the food is gone. Saving money is like rewarding yourself.

While young, you may want to invest your money into stocks, bonds or equipment. These things may help you later in life. Have a general plan for your life, with short term and long term goals. Make sure they are reasonable. It does no good to set a goal that you can never obtain. Pipe dreams and wish lists usually aren't all that helpful. The secret to success is found in the control of expenditures. Don't spend more than you make. Plan things out, and follow through.

-Car Maintenance-

Most generally changing a tire, and oil changes are the most prevalent problem situations.

-Oil Changes-

-<u>Regular oil changes</u> sometimes are offered with the purchase of a new car. Some dealers offer oil changes for the life of the car, however this sometimes isn't convenient for the owner. Usually, the oil change must be done at the dealership where the vehicle is purchased. This may prove to be difficult or impossible if the owner is out of town. Also, in the fine print of some of the offers, one may negate the offer if one or two regular oil changes are missed or not done at the right time or amount of miles.

Usually oil will need changed every three thousand to seventy-five hundred miles, depending on the oil. Some synthetics can go from ten to twenty thousand miles before needing changed. If one drives less than those number of miles a year, then an oil change is needed only once a year. On newer cars, a maintenance light will come on the dash that indicates an oil change is due. If a long term synthetic is used, this light will have to be turned off by an auto technician, or else simply just left on, knowing the reason for the light. Synthetic oil is far superior to regular oil in its ability to prevent wear and will increase the life expectancy of the engine.

If your car or truck isn't covered by any sort of oil change policy, then you may find a mechanic or oil change store to do it for you. If you simply want to save money, and have an interest in doing it yourself, it really isn't a difficult task and can usually take anywhere from twenty minutes to a half an hour. You will need certain tools for the job however. You will need paper towels for clean up, and probably a good soap for your hands. <u>Car ramps</u>- these may be purchased at a department store or autoparts store. The metal ones are best endurance wise. Carefully place the ramps in front of your vehicle so that they line up with the front tires. Slowly drive up the ramps and put the car in park. Turn the engine off.

You will also need to purchase a <u>wrench</u> the correct size as your oil pan drain plug. <u>A ratchet kit complete with sockets</u> is ideal for this. Most drain plugs are anywhere from thirteen millimeters, up to eighteen millimeters in size. Be careful not to confuse the oil drain pan with the transmission drain pan, which is part of the transmission. You will need to have <u>a drain pan</u> for the oil to drain out of the engine oil pan. Once the oil pan drain plug is removed, permit the oil to completely drain out into the flat pan that has been placed under it until it stops running and then stops dripping out. Once drained, one can remove the oil filter with the appropriate sized <u>oil filter wrench.</u> It is recommended that you use a good quality oil filter when you change your oil. Some are specifically made for synthetic oils and offer higher mile usage life. Once the oil is completely changed, put the drain plug back on and tighten it snuggly tight. Replace the oil filter with the new one, hand tight, only, but before doing that, you will need to put a dab of oil all around on the rubber seal of the oil filter. If the filter is put on too tightly, it may be impossible to take off next time, and have to be cut off. Once the oil filter is on and the drain plug is on tight, then put in the appropriate amount of oil by pouring it into the oil filler tube which is usually in the front, top part of the engine and sticks up with a cap on it. Most general rule of thumb an engine will take the number of quarts of oil as number of cylinders plus one half. So a four cylinder engine will usually take four and a half quarts, a six cylinder will take six and a half quarts. It is best to check with the owner's manual to be sure. Do not over-fill. Engine seals can be damaged, leak, or blown if the engine is pressured under a performance situation with more oil in it than it can handle.

While the hood is still up, check the condition of the air filter and replace if needed. Now is a good time to check other things as well such as taking the cap off the radiator and looking at the coolant and its level. Please be sure the radiator cap gets put back on securely. Also check the windshield washer and refill it if needed. One can usually see the brake fluid level in most modern cars and trucks that have semi-transparent reservoirs.

Once all the fluids have been checked and the oil has been properly filled, Pull the dip stick and see what level it reads. If okay, start the engine and let it run. Go around to the front of the vehicle and look under the engine area to see if there is any oil leaking from anywhere. If there are no oil leaks, then the hood may come down and the vehicle driven off the ramps. If the oil was over-filled, then the oil pan drain plug must be opened and the excess oil must be drained out to prevent engine damage. The old oil will need to be drained out of the oil drain pan that lies on the garage floor or on the driveway and placed into a disposable bottle such as a plastic milk bottle. That old oil should be taken to an oil reclaim station, garage, and some parts stores accept old oil. You will need to clean your hands off before getting back into the vehicle. In a day or two you should recheck the dip stick level to see if everything is still okay.

Once the vehicle has been pulled off the ramps and parked, turn the engine off. You are done except for the clean-up. Be sure you have not put grease or oil inside the car or steering wheel. Once you have done one oil change, any following oil changes will be quicker and easier than the first.

Changing a Tire.

This skill will absolutely be a plus to avoid being stranded. In order to help prevent having to change a tire at inconvenient times and places, carry in the trunk, tool box or glove box a can or two of "Fix-a Flat' or equivalent. This has been a "life saver" for many a would be stranded soul. In the case of a torn tire, sidewall damage, a cut or damaged valve stem, or rim damage, the "Fix-a-Flat" solution will not work, and therefore the tire must be changed. If the valve itself is the cause of the leak, it may easily be changed out in just a few minutes if another valve is available. Auto parts stores carry tire valves and a change out kit that will fit in most glove boxes. One may also be a member of a road side service such as Triple A. Some new cars come with road side service as part of their contract. Usually, new cars do not have much of any guarantee on the tires. Some states have state wide road side services on their interstate highways, but not on county roads.

If you find yourself broken down along the road, make sure your car is pulled well off the road, especially if you have a flat tire on the driver's side. The car should be on level ground to prevent a tip over. It is also a good idea to post cones or break-down warning triangles several hundred feet back away from your car as a warning. Road flares also may effectively be used especially at night. If at all possible do not park on a curve in the road, especially if warning signs of a breakdown are not placed Along this line, one also should include a first-aid kit in your car or truck in case you are ever hurt during an emergency.

To change a flat tire, please check to be sure you have a spare first. If you don't have a good spare, then, you may as well wait for a tow truck.

If you have a good spare tire, then, start by removing any center caps and or wheel covers. Some cars require a special tool for this, and if so it is usually supplied by the manufacturer. Mostly these are found either in the trunk, attached by a clip, or in the glove box, if there is one. Check your owner's manuel to see if a special tool is required. Please be careful not to lose the tool, but place it back in its storage area. Always check to see if that tool was placed back there if you have someone else change the tire. Garages are sometimes bad about returning the tool and leaving the owner stranded the next time. Just check. Usually just a screwdriver will work.

Take your lug wrench out of the trunk, or appropriately sized socket and breaker bar. If the lug nuts have been on there a long time and have been put on with an air gun, then, you may have to have a pipe extension to go over the handle of the wrench to break the lug nut loose. You will loosen the lug nuts one after another, in a star pattern. Star pattern means that you loosen one and then the next one to be loosened is directly across from it. Go in diagonals. You will need to tighten the lug nuts in the same pattern. Do not take the lug nuts off, just break them loose. If you take the lug nuts off at this time, the tire will want to just fall off and it may cause the jack to slip. You don't need the car to fall off the jack under any circumstances, so the lug nuts stay on until the car is jacked up so that the bottom of the flat tire leaves the ground. There should be a space of a couple of inches between the bottom of the flat tire and the ground.

An inflated tire will be larger than a deflated one, so there needs to be enough space under the flat tire to compensate for the inflated spare tire to go on. If not, you will have to jack the car up some more when the flat tire is off in order to put the spare on, which is not a good situation. If for any reason the jack slips while the flat is off and there's no wheel there at all, the vehicle could fall flat on the ground. Possible damage to the vehicle could occur if that happens. You will need a tow truck if the car is on the ground.

Once the flat is off, put the spare on and tighten the lug bolts on in the star pattern, being sure they are good and tight. Then lower the car back down so that it rests on the ground and put the flat in the trunk. Reinstall the wheel cover and or center cap. Put away all the tools, especially the wheel cover tool. Clean your hands off the best you can, and check to be sure there has been nothing left on the ground before closing the trunk. Check your clothing to be sure you aren't going to put dirt onto the upholstery. Once that is done, and all looks satisfactory, close the trunk and you are now free to go.

-Basic Plumbing-

Any truly serious problems, it is best get a plumber. Some apartment complexes have their own plumbers or those supplied by the owner, so check there at the office first.

If you find that you must do it yourself, make sure you turn the water off first. Some houses have a main shut off out near the street. Some homes have a water shut off for the different systems, like the toilet has a shut off valve on the pipe going into the water tank. If there is water leaking on the floor, go ahead and shut the water off even if you have called a plumber. It will cut down on the mess that needs cleaned up later. There often is a shut off valve that leads to the washing machine and also the dishwasher. The sooner the water is shut off, the less likely the chance of severe water damage. Get the water up as soon as possible. Sometimes water damage isn't actually seen until later when tile starts coming loose.

If you are dealing with a toilet, after you shut the water off, take the lid off the top and examine the situation. You may have to temporarily turn the water back on the inlet to see where the problem lies. Almost all toilet parts are sold at major outlets like Lowe's, Home Depot, and even Walmart. Replacement of these parts usually only takes a screwdriver and a pair of pliers. Take a good look at the part needed or take it with you when going out to get a replacement.

If the seat seal is faulty, there will be water seeping out from under the toilet. You will need a mop and a new toilet seal. The seal lies between the base of the toilet and the drain pipe in the floor. You will need to drain the toilet tank first, usually by just flushing it out of there. You will need to take the bolts off each side of the base seat with a wrench or pair of pliers and completely lift the toilet off the floor. Be careful not to lose the bolts. The area under the toilet needs thoroughly cleaned, and the old seal completely removed. Use a scraper if needed to remove and clean the place where the new seal will rest. After all the old seal has been completely removed and the drain pipe clean around its rim, place the new seal down around the outside of the drain pipe. It should be a snug fit. No adhesive is needed, and may actually case a leak. Carefully place the toilet seat back down on the new seal, being sure to let it straight down on it, and flat. Now reattach the toilet seat back to the floor with the bolts. Reconnect the tank, and turn the water back on. After the toilet has refilled, let it rest for a while. Clean up the floor and make it dry around the toilet so you can tell if it still leaks. Flush it and inspect for any leaks around the base or between the tank and seat. Seals do a good job, so if your repair was done carefully, there is a high probability of success with this task You have just saved a lot of money by doing it yourself. If you are uncertain about doing it yourself, get a friend to help you or get a plumber.

Leaky Faucets

Turn off the water to the faucet. Most sinks have a water shut off valve under the sink. Turning it clockwise (to the right) shuts the water off. Be sure it's turned off all the way. Once off, turn the faucet handles to let out the remaining water to help eliminate a water mess. You should buy what is called a plumber's wrench before starting. Sometimes there is a set screw that has a special fitting if the faucet is ceramic or some are even plastic. Use a flashlight or good moveable light to look both on top and under the countertop to see exactly what kind of fasteners are used. Most of these are tiny so a light may or may not be needed. You may not to take the faucet loose or off from underneath at all, some can be repaired just above the counter top. Even then, the water will still need turned off under the counter. After the repair is done, you will need to turn the faucets on, wide open, to let the air out of the line. If ther eis air in the line the water will "spit" out at first. This is normal. If you let the water run, the air will soon be gone and it will operate as normal.

Usually the washer that needs replaced can be accessed above the countertop, under the turn handles. There usually is a decorative cap on the top of the handle that can be removed to access a screw underneath. Some faucet handles can be removed by simply turning it in the opposite direction than what turns it on. Once the handle is off you will see as to whether the washer is replaceable or not. Some faucets brag that they are "washerless." That usually means the entire inside the housing will need replaced. They will come as one unit and can be found in the plumbing section of home repair stores.

If stumped, refer to the manufacturer's web site. Most faucets have the brand name stamped somewhere on the unit. If all else fails, the brand name is usually on the inside of the handle. Always check to see if you left air in the lines once you have worked repairing any water delivery system.

-Replace or Repairing Water Pipes

Water pipes can sprout a leak anywhere or at any time. Most often it is in the dead of winter due to a hard freeze. Letting a small stream of water run in a sink during below freezing weather will help prevent freeze ups and broken pipes. Prevention is the best of policies. If a pipe does break in the dead of winter, it is a very cold and huge mess. It also proves to be more difficult of a repair since you are also fighting the cold all dduring the repair time.

If you have copper tubing for pipes, you will need a butane torch to heat the ends to install a copper repair sleeve. A metal pipe cutter will also be needed to cut the copper pipe where it leaks so that the repair sleeve may be slipped on over it/ Once in place, heat the sleeve up with your torch. The heat will seal the sleeve to the pipe. Some repair sleeves require a flux to be applied so you probably need to check that before use. You may turn the water back on after it cools and check for leaks. A tubing bender is also recommended to have in your arsenal of tools if you have copper pipes and tubing.

Many modern houses have plastic pipes. If these crack or break, you will need to cut the plastic pipe with a pipe cutter or even a hacksaw will do. A plastic repair sleeve is needed. If you have to cut away a section of plastic pipe, you will need two repair sleeves and section of new plastic pipe of the same size. Plastic pipe has its size stamped right on it so there's little chance of mistakes. Plastic pipe glue is also required. This usually comes with an applier inside the lid. Read the glue label to be sure it works with the kind of plastic your pipe is made of. Make sure the old pipe is clean and generously apply the glue to the inside and outside of the pipe and sleeve. Push the two ends together and it will automatically seal. This plastic glue takes just a short time to dry so you may turn the water on in a short period of time. Check for leaks. There will be air in the line, so all the faucets effected will need to be turned on for a while to force the air out of the line. Water "spitting" out at first is normal. If you leave the water run, the spitting will soon stop, and it will return to normal operation shortly.

-Wood Working Projects

I have found that both boys and girls enjoy making simple things out of

wood. These are good projects for interaction. A simple two or three piece book shelf that is hand sanded makes a nice memory of accomplishment. The adult can work the saw or deal with the more difficult and dangerous part of the endeavor. Depending on the age, the youth may enjoy the assembly and or painting of the project.

Some tools for wood working are necessary: hammers, saws of various kinds, sandpaper, and/or a sander, fasteners and /or glue, a wood square, a measuring device. The age and ability of the youth needs to be considered in the difficulty of the project. Start simple and work on more time consuming, complicated projects later as skills build. A child or youth should never be left alone in a shop with power tools. Even the most skilled of craftsmen get injured on occasion. You will need a first aid kit handy, just in case. Safety first is the rule. Don't take chances. Shortcuts may be shortcuts to disaster.

Some easy projects for the beginner may be:

1. A cutting board for the kitchen.
2. A wood bench.
3. A simple rack for magazines or books.
4. Hand-made serving trays.
5. Shoe storage box and booster stool.
6. An outdoor wood bench with back.
7. Coat or hat rack
8. A spice rack
9. A wall book rack
10. Book Ends.

11 Decorative wall ornament

Terms:

1. Cross Cut- is to cut the board across the grain
2. Rip Cut is cutting with the grain- or in the same direction the grain goes.
3. A Square Cut is a ninety degree cut to the edge of the wood.
4. A Miter Cut is any non-ninety degree cut to the edge of the wood
5. A Bevel Cut is any non-ninety degree cut in regard to the surface of the wood.
6. Finish- either the stain or paint applied to a wood's surface.
7. Butt Joint- two pieces of wood connected together at either a ninety or one-eighty degree angle.

8. Miter Joints- two forty-five degree angled cuts to joint two pieces of wood together.
9. Edge Joint- joins two edges together with fasteners.
10. Kerf- the width of cut the saw makes in the wood.
11. Router- a power tool used to cut grooves in wood, and form shapes.

Also, consider what kind of wood that you want for your project. The most commonly used wood is pine. Pine is considered a soft wood, but is easy to work with and inexpensive compared to the other woods. For special projects you may select a special wood such as cherry or maple. Pine can be stained to look like just about any other wood. There is also what is called "wood fill," It is a putty that can be used to cover unwanted drilled holes or unsightly small cracks. Cracks in wood are not harmful as long as it is in a non-stressed use. Cracked wood should not be used in any load bearing usage such as in ladders or ramps.

-Cooking-

This is a necessary skill that many young people attempt to avoid. Some level of mastery of essentials are necessary in order to survive, because fast food and even restaurant eating can get old.

Even before you set up to cook, be sure your food has been properly stored. Canned foods last a long time but not forever. Check the dates. Usually if the contents have gone bad inside, the can will look like it's ready to explode, or it may even begin leaking. Food processors do not process the canned food to last as long in a can as they once did, so the shelf life may not be what you think it is. If you want a long term storage of food, it probably is best to go with dried goods such as dried beans or dried peas in a bag. Rice should be frozen before put on the shelf for storage. This kills any thing that may have been living in it. Afterwards, you may safely lay in on a shelf in the pantry. Before cooking, always rinse the rise off to remove foreign particles. Dried foods are best stored in sealable containers or buckets.

The basic cooking methods today are: frying, baking, microwave, boiling, slow cook crockpots, Instapots, and pressure cookers. In many cases you will find that the package that contains the food will have suggestions on "how to cook" printed right on it. Once you have done these suggestions, you may want to experiment with the ingredients to suit your own taste. Also, there are many good cook books on the market, so it is probably a good idea to have one purchased for your use in the kitchen. The most universal are the large ones that have removable pages. Good cooking ideas with instructions, pictures and even videos can be also found on the internet. Just type in "How to cook _____" and you will find that there usually are many good ways to cook the food you have in mind.

Remember, the fresher the better. Also, home grown vegetables are always better than store bought. Store purchased veggies often are "water grown" with little or no fertilizer. Lacking nutrients, the fruit or vegetable will have little or no taste. It may be juicy (or not) but the juice is more water than anything. Store bought fruits and vegetables also may have artificial coloring added to make it look ripe, when in reality it was picked early and isn't even close to being ripe. Store purchased fruit and vegetables may also retain the poison of pesticides on them or even in them, so be sure to wash them thoroughly. Home grown can eliminate this problem. Even an indoor box that sits near a window can serve as a vegetable garden. If you go this route, you may want to buy fruit that has seeds that can be planted. Some fruits that have seeds have been modified so that the seed won't grow even if planted. Be sure to wash thoroughly anything that is planted, because tiny bugs may live on the surface.

Also, one may choose to enhance skills in the kitchen by viewing various chiefs on television. Usually their programs are entertaining was well as educational. Even cooks with years of experience should be open to new ideas. A good cook will always look for ways of getting even better.

Safety in the kitchen is number one. Some things to look out for are:

1. Never walk away for long periods or leave the house with the stove burners on.
2. . When the stove is not in use, it should have nothing resting on it.
3. Be sure the burners are clean and clear of old grease. Grease fires are probably the number one cause of kitchen fires in the U.S..
4. . Keep a fire extinguisher near the stove. Make sure it is in working order.
5. . Keep ovens clean. Anything spilled in an oven will possibly cause serious smoke and set off fire alarms.
6. Keep refrigerators clean so that stored foods aren't contaminated.
7. Have "oven mittens" near the stove or oven. Aprons will keep grease, flour and other kitchen items off your clothes, so it is

best to wear one.

Keep the kitchen clean is the major rule. Cleanliness is key to having a good food product. This is the reason the government has food inspectors go around and check restaurant cleanliness among other things. Their score must be posted to the public, with a one hundred being the best. Anything below the nineties is a reason for concern for the customer that something isn't being run right. If you don't properly store your food, and you don't keep your counters and floors clean, you are inviting infestation. Once bugs start inhabiting, it may be difficult and expensive to get rid of them. Usually, the best time to exterminate is at night. Usually a professional pest control company doesn't exterminate completely, but controls. It is good for business to have a problem threatening. So if the bugs are gone, thanks to your pest control agent, he will be sure to stick around with his contract to see to it that they stay gone. Use your own good judgment in your choices of pest control companies if you decide you need one.

Tips on Buying a Home or Getting an Apartment.

Probably the first and most important consideration in getting either a house or an apartment is how much can you afford? How much have you saved for this project? Home buying, especially first time home buyers, usually need a large down payment to secure a loan for the house. This may be at least twenty percent of the cost of the house. Down payments are higher if your credit isn't so good. If you are considering renting an apartment, you will find that most require anywhere from one to three month's rent in advance, and a security deposit that supposedly will be refunded if and when you decide to move. Any perceived damages to the property will result in no refund, and you may be charged for any repairs. The poorer your credit the more money you will have to save in advance of such an endeavor. Remember a house requires insurance also. It needs utilities to be paid once a month to keep it livable. New, first timers will need furniture and appliances, also. Sometimes, pre-fab homes, double wide trailers and house trailers may offer the best option for your money, depending on your finances and needs. They usually come equipped with appliances and even furnished. A used one or a repo may be the answer to those who have less to offer in finances.

Once you have determined that you indeed can afford to get either a house or apartment, then you will need to figure out its hypothetical location. For this you may want to consult a real estate agent. Shop for mortgages. Traditionally, spring is home buying season. Inspect the house of hire someone to do that for you. You may want to negotiate any needed repairs with the seller against the price. If you have children, you may consider the schools in the area. Are they good schools? If not children are involved, then consider how close a place is to stores and your place of employment. What are the property taxes like? What kind of neighborhood is the prospective place in? Best to stay out of high crime areas even though the rent may be lower. You and your friends, and family's safety depends on what kind of neighborhood you move into.

You may have to stay at the first place you move to for a long time, so use good judgment in your move.

6.
Counselling.

First of all let it be said that children with serious psychological, and sociological problem need to be referred to a professional. Before we can do this, however, we need to be able to recognize that there is a problem. Sadly, some parents, and even some teachers overlook these things instead of dealing with them. Ignoring the problem won't help it go away. We also must keep in mind that the longer the problem is permitted to exist, usually the worse it gets. Sometimes just a word of advice is all that is needed, but other times, further follow-up is needed.

When dealing with a possible problem in a child we tend to put certain behaviors into three basic categories.

1. Developmental Problems- this includes such things as clumsiness, language problems, seizures, sexual problems, sleeping problems, stunted maturing,
2. Psychopatholical Problems- this hyperactivity, conduct disturbance, academic problems, psychosis.
3. Psycho-social Problems- family problems as well as school relationships.

Learning about a child's problems will involve the family as well as friends of the child. A child may not even recognized that they have a problem, so some of the information gathering should be from family and friends. Usually it is best to see and question the child first, then the family separately, then all together. Because a child has a symptom doesn't necessarily mean there is a serious problem. Serious psychological problems are indicated by multiple symptoms. The more symptoms, the more serious the problem the child may have. Also to be considered is the severity of the symptom. Finally, the symptoms duration and frequency. All these factors must be considered in your initial assessment. Let it also be known that the removal of a symptom doesn't necessarily mean the underlying problem has been solved.

Procedure of Examining the Child and Family:

1. Gather information about the child: age, interests, hobbies, etc.
2. Gather information about the family; housing, finances, health, any criminal background, family's attitude toward child.
3. Obtain a history of the child's problem/s from past teachers, family.
4. Examination of the child is critical:

   a. General appearance and attitude.
   b. Motor function- hyperactive, or underactive, writing abilities, clumsy, quick or slow.
   c. Speech- articulate, slow of speech, stutters, disjointed speech.
   d. Sees things that don't exist- not pretending.
   e. Knowledge of surroundings, people's names, time and date. Alertness.
   f. Appearance of social adjustment- has friends, gets along well in school.

Examination of Parents:

   a. Note the interaction between parents
   b. Note the attitude of the parents toward the child (accepting, rejecting, anxious, consistent, protective, disinterested, tolerant, overprotective, etc.)
   c. Who does the child confide in?

    d. Who is the main caretaker of the child?

Ask the parent what they feel should be done about the problem, and proceed from there. An administrator should be involved in any one of these examinations or conferences. Then, go with what is recommended by the administration. If the parent is acting on their own, then it is usually best to go with what a trusted professional recommends. A second opinion sometimes is reassuring.

7.
Suggested Reading

Please Note: many of these books and other resources are available on line

Childhood Development:

Essentials of Practice-Based Coaching: Supporting Effective Practices in Early Childhood 1st Edition

by Dr. Patricia Snyder Ph.D.[1] (Author), Dr. Lise Fox Ph.D.[2] Brooks Publishing, 2021, 304 pages.

The Educator's Guide to Understanding Child Development

By Linda Mayes[3], Scholastic Teaching Resources, 192 Pages.

Early Start Denver Model for Young Children with Autism: Promoting Language, Learning, and Engagement Illustrated Edition

by Sally J. Rogers[4] (Author), Geraldine Dawson[5] (Author); The Guilford Press, 2009; 297 Pages.

Parent Training for Disruptive Behavior: The RUBI Autism Network, Clinician Manual (Programs That Work), by Karen

---

1. https://www.amazon.com/s/ref=dp_byline_sr_book_1?ie=UTF8&field-author=Dr.+Patricia+Snyder+Ph.D.&text=Dr.+Patricia+Snyder+Ph.D.&sort=relevancerank&search-alias=books
2. https://www.amazon.com/s/ref=dp_byline_sr_book_2?ie=UTF8&field-author=Dr.+Lise+Fox+Ph.D.&text=Dr.+Lise+Fox+Ph.D.&sort=relevancerank&search-alias=books
3. https://shop.scholastic.com/parent-ecommerce/search-results.html?text=Linda%20Mayes
4. https://www.amazon.com/Sally-J-Rogers/e/B001JP88NQ/ref=dp_byline_cont_book_1
5. https://www.amazon.com/s/ref=dp_byline_sr_book_2?ie=UTF8&field-author=Geraldine+Dawson&text=Geraldine+Dawson&sort=relevancerank&search-alias=books

Bearss[6] (Author), Cynthia R. Johnson[7] (Author), Oxford University Press; August 2018; 248 Pages.

EARLY CHILDHOOD DEVELOPMENT: PREBIRTH THROUGH AGE EIGHT By Sandra Anselmo Mint; Prentice Hall; 1994, 574 Pages.

Positive Discipline for Teenagers, Revised 3rd Edition: Empowering Your Teens and Yourself Through Kind and Firm Parenting; by Jane Nelsen[8] (Author), Lynn Lott[9] (Author); ; Harmony; August 14, 2012; 272 Pages.

Good Inside: A Practical Guide to Becoming the Parent You Want to be – September 15, 2022, by Becky Kennedy[10] (Author); Thorsons; Sept. 2020; 304 Pages.

Prevent, Teach, Reinforce for Young Children: The Early Childhood Model of Individualized Positive Behavior Support, New edition by Glen Dunlap Ph.D.[11] (Author), Kelly Wilson B.S.[12] (Author); Brooks Publishing; Feb. 2022; 248 Pages.

---

6. https://www.amazon.com/s/ref=dp_byline_sr_book_1?ie=UTF8&field-author=Karen+Bearss&text=Karen+Bearss&sort=relevancerank&search-alias=books

7. https://www.amazon.com/s/ref=dp_byline_sr_book_2?ie=UTF8&field-author=Cynthia+R.+Johnson&text=Cynthia+R.+Johnson&sort=relevancerank&search-alias=books

8. https://www.amazon.com/Jane-Nelsen/e/B001H6RSL0/ref=dp_byline_cont_book_1

9. https://www.amazon.com/s/ref=dp_byline_sr_book_2?ie=UTF8&field-author=Lynn+Lott&text=Lynn+Lott&sort=relevancerank&search-alias=books

10. https://www.amazon.com/Becky-Kennedy/e/B09LVW3JGZ/ref=dp_byline_cont_book_1

11. https://www.amazon.com/Glen-Dunlap-Ph-D/e/B07HL8KH6G/ref=dp_byline_cont_book_1

The 7 Habits of Highly Effective Teenagers Paperback, by Sean Covey, Simon and Shuster; January 1, 2016, 218 Pages.

Master Your Destiny: A Practical Guide to Rewrite Your Story and Become the Person You Want to Be (Personal Workbook) by Thibaut Meurisse[13], Mastery Series, February 14, 2020; 100 Pages.

---

12. https://www.amazon.com/s/ref=dp_byline_sr_book_2?ie=UTF8&field-author=Kelly+Wilson&text=Kelly+Wilson+B.S.&sort=relevancerank&search-alias=books

13. https://www.amazon.com/Thibaut-Meurisse/e/B014BHILJE/ref=dp_byline_cont_book_1

Reading

Teaching Reading Sourcebook (Core Literacy Library) Third Edition; by Bill Honig[1] (Author) by, Linda Diamond[2] (Author), Linda Gutlohn[3] (Author), Academic Therapy Publications; Sept. 2018; 848 Pages.

The Reading Strategies Book 2.0: Your Research-Based Guide to Developing Skilled Readers 1st Edition; by Jennifer Serravallo[4] (Author); Heinemann Pub. Jan. 2023; 480 Pages.

The New Art and Science of Teaching Reading (How to Teach Reading Comprehension Using a Literacy Development Model) (The New Art and Science of Teaching Book Series) Illustrated Edition; by Julia A. Simms[5] (Author), Robert J. Marzano[6] (Author); Solution Tree Press, Aug. 2018;

224 Pages.

---

1. https://www.amazon.com/s/ref=dp_byline_sr_book_1?ie=UTF8&field-author=Bill+Honig&text=Bill+Honig&sort=relevancerank&search-alias=books
2. https://www.amazon.com/s/ref=dp_byline_sr_book_2?ie=UTF8&field-author=Linda+Diamond&text=Linda+Diamond&sort=relevancerank&search-alias=books
3. https://www.amazon.com/Linda-Gutlohn/e/B0CRYBWJGJ/ref=dp_byline_cont_book_3
4. https://www.amazon.com/Jennifer-Serravallo/e/B003N776K4/ref=dp_byline_cont_book_1
5. https://www.amazon.com/Julia-A-Simms/e/B00E6X65LU/ref=dp_byline_cont_book_1
6. https://www.amazon.com/Robert-J-Marzano/e/B001HPOO54/ref=dp_byline_cont_book_2

Abeka Basic Phonics Charts (Grades 1-3; New Edition);

Abeka Publishers / 2016

Foundations Phonics: Easy Lessons for Early Learners, By: Carrie Lindquist[7]

Master Books / 2016; 334 Pages.

CVC Phonics Flash Cards for Preschool and Kindergarten - 130 Sight Words, Vocabulary Building, Educational Teaching Aids, Mixed Color Paper Cards for Homeschool Supplies.by Funny Learning. Order through Temu; 2024.

Beginning Reading Comprehension for Kindergarten Workbook: Sight Words Reading Passages with Comprehension Questions for Emergent Readers by J Ecochardt[8], Comprehension Builders, November 22, 2023, 67 Pages.

You may want to shop for reading books and story books on line for the reading level your child has obtained. Encourage reading by reading books yourself. It shows that it is a worthwhile thing to do.

---

7. https://www.christianbook.com/apps/easyfind?Ntk=author&Ntt=Carrie%20Lindquist

8. https://www.amazon.com/J-Ecochardt/e/B0CNY7P71Q/ref=dp_byline_cont_book_1

Cooking

The Science-Backed Mediterranean Diet Cookbook for Beginners with Colored Pictures, by Elena Florenz[1]; Independent Publishers, September 2024, 113 Pages.

The Pillsbury Cookbook: The All-Purpose Companion for Today's Cook Paperback, by the Pillsbury Company; March 1, 1996; 928 pages.

How to Cook Everything: 2,000 Simple Recipes for Great Food, 10th Anniversary Edition Hardcover, by Mark Bittman[2] Houghton Mifflin Harcourt; October 3, 2008, 1056 Pages.

Mastering the Art of French Cooking (2 Volume Set) Hardcover – Box set, by Julia Child[3] (Author), Louisette Bertholle[4]; Knopf, December 1, 2009.

The Mexican Home Kitchen: Traditional Home-Style Recipes That Capture the Flavors and Memories of Mexico Hardcover – Illustrated, by Mely Martínez[5]; Rock Point; September 15, 2020, 192 Pages

---

1. https://www.amazon.com/Elena-Florenz/e/B0DHTP7M6F/ref=dp_byline_cont_book_1

2. https://www.amazon.com/Mark-Bittman/e/B000APUJB0/ref=dp_byline_cont_book_1

3. https://www.amazon.com/Julia-Child/e/B000AQ0XXS/ref=dp_byline_cont_book_1

4. https://www.amazon.com/s/ref=dp_byline_sr_book_2?ie=UTF8&field-author=Louisette+Bertholle&text=Louisette+Bertholle&sort=relevancerank&search-alias=books

5. https://www.amazon.com/Mely-Mart%C3%ADnez/e/B08B761P7S/ref=dp_byline_cont_book_1

SIMPLE CLASSICS COOKBOOKWILLIAMS-Sonoma Complete Cookbooks, Chuck Williams, Oxmoor House; January 2002; 304 Pages.

Automotive Repair

Auto Repair and Maintenance by Dave Stribling, Penguin Random House, 2015, 282 Pages.

The Care Care Book, by Ron Haefner, Delmar Learning, 2004, 443 Pages.

Haynes Repair Manual. Application specific. Order on line or pick up at a auto parts store. –detailed and up to date.

How to Buy a Home:

HOW TO BUY A HOUSE: What Everyone Should Know Before They Buy or Sell a Home Paperback, by Mark Ferguson, Independent Publisher, May 10, 2017, 318 Pages.

Balancing the Family Budget

HOW TO ADULT: PERSONAL Finance for the Real World Paperback, by Jake Cousineau. Independently Published, March 23, 2021, 235 Pages.

Game Rule Books

The Official Rules of Baseball Illustrated : An Irreverent Look at the Rules of Baseball and How They Came to Be What They Are Today (Paperback), by David Nemec; Sports Publishing, 2020, 360 Pages

Football Rules Illustrated, by George Sullivan, Simon and Schuster; 1985, 196 Pages.

Soccer Rules and Regulations, by Clive Gifford, Power Kids; 2010, 32 Pages.

Official Rules of Volleyball Paperback, by United States Volleyball Association[1], Triumph Books; 1994, 192 Pages.

Official Pickle Ball Rule Book, by U.S.A. Pickle Ball Association, 2024-25.

How to Win at Chess: The Ultimate Guide for Beginners and Beyond, Hardcover –Levy Rozman, Ten Speed Press, October 24, 2023, 272 Pages.

Bobby Fischer Teaches Chess ,Paperback – Bantam by Bobby Fischer[2]

July 1, 1982, 352 Pages. Learn from the Greatest of All Time.

---

1. https://www.amazon.com/s/ref=dp_byline_sr_book_1?ie=UTF8&field-author=United+States+Volleyball+Association&text=United+States+Volleyball+Association&sort=relevancerank&search-alias=books

2. https://www.amazon.com/Bobby-Fischer/e/B001HD393Y/ref=dp_byline_cont_book_1

Field Hockey for Beginners: The Ultimate Guide to Mastering Everything from Rules, Sticks, and Etiquette to Ball Control, Shooting, and Goalkeeping by Cade Hill, (Learning Sports), September 19, 2023, 92 Pages.

General

How to Adult: An Illustrated Guide, by Stephen Wildish, Source Books, 2023, 192 Pages. This gives a humorous perspective on adult life and its problems.

Books to be Read to or by Young People:

Aesop's Fables, by G.F. Townsend, Routledge and Sons, London, Reprint 2012. 192 Pages.

My Very First Mother Goose Hardcover – Illustrated, by Iona Opie[1] (Author), Rosemary Wells[2] (Illustrator), Candlwick, September 27, 2016, 108 Pages.

Nursery Rhymes & Learning Toys for Toddlers 1-3, Talking Song Books & Musical Books for Boys & Girls, The Astro Learns Series Publisher, 2024, 35 Pages.

I Can Read! Readers - Level 1 Series of 12 different books in a package, easy readers for Kindergarten and first grade levels, by Lakeshore Publishers, 2024.

Check out the Lakeshore web site for books at reasonable prices for children of all ages and grade levels. E-Bay and Amazon has great deals on bulk purchases as well as baughmans-books.myshopify.com offers books for different age levels also.

---

1. https://www.amazon.com/Iona-Opie/e/B000APA6ZY/ref=dp_byline_cont_book_1
2. https://www.amazon.com/s/ref=dp_byline_sr_book_2?ie=UTF8&field-author=Rosemary+Wells&text=Rosemary+Wells&sort=relevancerank&search-alias=books

Post Script

I have written this book with the hopes of perhaps helping someone, even if a little, in their life experiences. We all ought to be willing to help others along the way. Sometimes just knowing the rules is enough. You do this with your children or grandchildren, and if a teacher, you daily help your students with guidance and advice. Your efforts can be greatly appreciated and rewarded in many ways. Just like our parents and grandparents before us, we often forget who helped us with something along the way. In these cases, not even so much as a thank you is given or received. Just to be able to view a child or another person being successful in what you helped them with is in itself rewarding. This is really what education is about, and ultimately what life is all about: helping one another to make a better world. Prayers and best wishes to all my readers, hoping for your much success along the way. Never tire of doing good things for others, as well as for yourself. Living only for yourself is a lonely life, so I recommend a life of sharing what you know and do with others that which is beneficial.

Thank you.

Dr. Myron Baughman

The End

Don't miss out!

Visit the website below and you can sign up to receive emails whenever Myron Baughman publishes a new book. There's no charge and no obligation.

https://books2read.com/r/B-A-CJJBB-VQMJF

BOOKS 2 READ

Connecting independent readers to independent writers.

Did you love *The Practical Resource Book*? Then you should read *The Wizard's Haunted Castle Mystery*[1] by Myron Baughman!

International Investigator Zeb Dasher takes a difficult, haunted castle case and finds the clues to be deceptive to the end.

Read more at https://www.sermonaudio.com/source_detail.asp?sourceid=kingjamesseminary.

---

1. https://books2read.com/u/bOqX10
2. https://books2read.com/u/bOqX10

Also by Myron Baughman

Pneumasites
Pneumasites 2

The Learning Series
The Practical Resource Book

Zeb Dasher Mystery Novels
The Twisted Case of the Presidential Conspiracy
The Wizard's Haunted Castle Mystery

Standalone
Pneumasites
Educating Everett
My Puppy Theo
Trixie: The Pixie Angel
The Ghosts of Griswoldville

Watch for more at https://www.sermonaudio.com/source_detail.asp?sourceid=kingjamesseminary.

About the Author

Dr. Myron Baughman is a graduate of Bob Jones University with a degree of B.S. in Education. His Th.M is from the International Bible Seminary. He graduated with honors from the Andersonville Theological Seminary. Myron and his wife Denise live in Georgia and have four children. Myron is a published author and serves as the President of the King James Bible Seminary.

Read more at https://www.sermonaudio.com/source_detail.asp?sourceid=kingjamesseminary.

www.ingramcontent.com/pod-product-compliance
Ingram Content Group UK Ltd.
Pitfield, Milton Keynes, MK11 3LW, UK
UKHW042154171224
452513UK00001B/92